FOR JAY

*Nothing would give up life:*

*Even the dirt kept breathing a small breath.*

THEODORE ROETHKE

*There are no stars tonight*

*But those of memory.*

*Yet how much room for memory there is ...*

HART CRANE

# ACKNOWLEDGEMENTS

My thanks to the editors of the following, where ver-
sions of many of these poems have appeared :

*Ariel*

*CBC Radio*

*Dandelion*

*Grain*

*Literary Review of Canada*

*Prairie Fire*

*Sanscrit*

*Studio Café Anthology*

*Tributes in Verse – A Poetry Now Anthology (U.K.)*

*Wascana Review*

*Women's Television Network*


Thank you to my loving sister Susan who never lets
me take the easy way out.

A special thank you to my editor and dear friend,
Christopher Wiseman, without whom this book
would not exist.

# TABLE OF CONTENTS

# PART ONE

*Linda Lovelace Please Tell Me Your Name*

## ONE OF THEM

Outside my window children pass on
their way to school. In my warm
purple housecoat, with my hot
white mug of coffee,
I remember passing on my way
to school not looking
in the windows either. Grownups
in old bathrobes, brown
mouths, and all the sad red
pullings under their eyes.

## MRS. BERNIE WON

The quiet death of me
in grade three arithmetic, word problems.
Peaches were too squishy for words.
Apples sliced into fractions,
but wouldn't fit in my pies.
In the front of the class
Mrs. Bernie sat at her desk shaking me,
her arm fat jiggling my thinness.
It was summertime.
The poplars quivered.

My legs teetered back to my seat,
past rows of desks neat as hate.
Past Marion Fisher eagerly
picking her nose.
My self lost,
I found my place in the lesson,
shame, my new companion.

Mrs. Bernie's dress was covered
in mosquito small flowers,
tiny biters that stung when she barked,
*Stupid girl, stupid stupid girl.*

The shaking did not hurt.
My self slid gently to the cool grey floor.
Outside a few pine needles fell.

## WHY MY FATHER WATCHES MY HANDS

Often it drives my Dad crazy
to watch me iron, wrap gifts,
wash dishes. His mouth starts going,
he makes small grunting sounds,
his hands begin miming mine,
or he just takes over.
*Let the master do it.*

Grampa had hands.
Brown leather and stiff.
They didn't close all the way
around your fingers,
but he could drive a car
and hold a drink.
He had both elbows.

All those years Dad strapped
and unstrapped his father's hands,
cut his meat, watched for enemies.
He wanted him to wear hooks instead —
*Much more efficient. He could smoke
a pipe again, even light matches.*

Grampa said no,
they would scare the children,
distress the women.

He had both elbows. In 1912
his hands brushed live wires
putting up power lines in Saskatchewan.
My Great-Uncle Bill, strongest,
shortest man in Eastend,
had to be held back by five men
when he saw his brother burning.

## Stained

Country Time Doughnuts is empty.

*Freshly Made Coffee For Every Cup,*
Maybe, but they don't have sour
cream cake doughnuts, I see
that right away.

Now I try not to see the waitress
has a port-wine stain
splash. It is cold November
and she wears an off-the-shoulder
top accentuating her colours.

I think of all the times
I spilled the last mouthfulls
of coffee on my desk, and how far it rolls
through papers, books and on
down table legs and deep into the carpet.

I choose carefully, nothing with red
jam. I smile sympathetically too.
She's pissed off at how long

I'm taking and meets my smiles
with angry chews of her frittered
fingernails and slow rolls
of her small almond eyes.

I want things
coffee and doughnut simple.
But here I am,
a real pain in the ass. I get it
from my mother.

She's the one white woman
who sits next to the one
black person on the bus
even when the bus is empty.

I keep smiling,
pointing to wrong doughnuts,
knowing the red
is rising in my cheeks.

# STAINED GLASS WINDOWS *(For Kathleen)*

1.

Jesus,

all cut up,

filters your morning light:

Victorian red,

water-green,

molten amber.


His is the first face

you see each day you wake

and have those few seconds

of forgetting.


Once a week I wake,

turn my face to a blank wall,

and don't move a muscle, quietly

imagining I'm you.


2.

I didn't know you well then.

I didn't like you much either.

I was mad about your brother.

On picnics
You leapt mountains,
scaled rock faces,
while we lagged
behind mortal and slow.
(And look at you, even now,
sailing past me down the hall
in your motorized chair.)

In the evenings,
cornered by fire-light
you'd recite "Hiawatha" breathless
and haughty to adoring fellows
on ships from Harvard or Yale.
Later they'd drown
in love for you.

You were at ease everywhere.
I only pretended to be
and kept my distance.

3.
I'm not going to say it.
So damn easy to say it.

4.

Out for dinner, we look
smashing, sipping champagne
cocktails, flirting shamelessly
with married waiters, cracking
secrets.

The next morning,
after sleeping over,
we wake
blurry-eyed, dreamy,
and I hold a glass
of bright orange juice to your lips.

Oh Kathleen — the soft ache
of full sun on our lives.

## L I N D A  L O V E L A C E

Sitting on the edge
of my mother's single bed,
flipping through the channels
of her small black and white T.V.
I heard your name. I knew it from
"Deep Throat" jokes the boys told every time
one of us licked our lips too happily.

I ogled you, six months pregnant, all warm
motherly breasts and thick black braids
on either side of your soft face.
I was sixteen and you were infamous.

Joyce Davidson, the rat blonde host
in the tattletale suit squeaked
back to the same question.
*But how did you do it?*
*It was a muscle trick.*

She wanted more.
She wanted specifics. You
wanted specifics too:
how a gun was held to your temple

and your family threatened
so you would do the throat trick properly.
How you were raped and beaten
and beaten and raped so many times
that this child would be the only one
your womb could hold.

The host scurried to find the exact
muscles you used to hold down penises
in your torn throat. She couldn't
hide her little pink tongue as she asked,
*Can anyone do it?*

Linda Lovelace what is your name?
I know his name, the one who made the films,
the one who slept on top of you
for two years, watched through a hole
in the door each time you went to the toilet,
watched you bleed and break
over and over, as easily as watching
re-runs of the "Dating Game,"
and who did no time for what he did.

Linda Lovelace please tell me your name.
Linda Lovelace don't if you don't want to.

## CONTAGION

She seeps through sometimes
when I slice a boneless
chicken breast, make love
to my husband, see children
play tag and I tighten tighten
sure as this bizarre word
I never heard before
cuts on my teeth
— nun-chucks .

I caught the last
eight minutes of Oprah:
women who killed their spouses
acquitted because of years of abuse.

Her hair dense black, lips pretty pulpy
broken nose-memory no scarlet scars
dark eyes sleepless bruisy soft.

He called himself Storm Shadow.
Thought he was a ninja as he kicked
and punched her two small children.
Used these nun-chucks and her as slaves —
heavy metal chains with hardwood ends

breaking skin and bone as he raped
her ten year old four or five times
a day so she would conceive
his ninja fetus.

She took two kitchen knives one day
and stabbed and stabbed
and two days later he died
and it was over.

I have no knives and now
my gentle husband handles
a wife who tightens
tightens like a captured slave.
Ninjas and nun-chucks
words and numbers
beat beat beat —

8 minutes
4 or 5 times a day
10 years old
Storm Shadow
nun-chucks ready
crayons scattered
2 knives —
Over and over
never over.

## I Was Drawn to Her

The first time I thought of a bird,
Or a beaten-down yellow feather.
Dried out, hungry, khaki-eyed,
She never spoke.

Smiling at reassuring intervals,
(Not too much),
My eyes always lowered,
I watched her.

The second time she wore a wrist cast,
Her tiny eyes scribbling volumes.
God she must have seen unspeakable red . . .
Has kept silent out of fear.

By the third meeting she was speaking,
A well modulated, educated voice.
I liked her almost as much.
At the fourth meeting she broke down.

A mother of two, college professor,
Should have known better —

We all nodded.

She broke her son's arm once,

Sent both kids to the hospital two, three times,

Begged their forgiveness.

Afterward, reptilian, I hugged her.

Through the fifth meeting she was by my side,

Freshly bathed, well fed, eagle-eyed.

Long elegant hands fondled chocolate wafers.

She offered me one.

I declined.

## BED TIME *(for Lisa)*

Like clams her hands
lock in prayer:
small pink beggars
against the dark.

The Sandman will pry open
squirming memories —
Daddy catching her;
sticky pyjamas.

Her eyes search my face:
huge blue gapers
caught on hooks,
shark deep,
they won't close.

Glassy-eyed.
Terrified.
On her salt bed
she'll weep him out
for me to catch.

## BUOYANCY

Dirty girl on the beach
in Belize didn't own a bath
and asked to have one with me.

And I bathed with you girl
in that four-footed tub
when you followed me home
past the terraced café
where dark waiters white-gloved
smiling brought me coffee
ice cream Mummy mashed for me.
Past the docks where Daddy and I fished
sweet carp and felt the ocean
through conch shells.

My parents dunked their daughter
in water with you —
coffee-coloured like my best treat,
sharing your fat-cheeked glee
as we played tag with soap foam.

In the bubbles
we didn't have breasts
but you said we'd get them
gigglesplash splash splash.

I never saw you again.

When I was seven I bathed
with Barbie but she wouldn't float
so I had to rip her head off —
it floated fine.

Now I have breasts and bathe
alone too much.

## In Heat

The Louthouds
(Latoots, my father calls them)
have a brown cockerspaniel named Toy.
Sometimes she appears diapered
in sheets, brown blood splotches
on her white belly, legs scrambling
four ways at once.
In heat is what they say.
I don't ask questions.
In heat is what I am,
full of hot
eight year old self-hate at Joy Haskel's
(my father calls them Rascals)
birthday party.

Joy —
ten years old with woman's hips,
body smells, and lingerie I don't like.

Joy —

child-star smiling,

about to burst not in soft pieces

but in hard candy cracks,

announces Kentucky Fried Chicken for lunch.


Joy's father is in heat —

the bucket of chicken

squat between his legs.

The parade of party dresses

snaps to attention:

ALL DARK MEAT LOVERS LINE UP LEFT

ALL WHITE MEAT LOVERS LINE UP RIGHT


In heat my legs slowly wander.

In heat his mouth spits

PICK A LINE


In heat I say I don't care.

In heat I ate white meat.

I hate white meat.

## Our Parents Met On A Plane

No plants in that house
but a garden with a bad cat
called Princess gnawing chicken
legs until blood was bitten through bone —
the way I felt at Madeleine's home,
locked in her mother's hot lipstick hello,
red and yellow paint on wooden dolls,
red and white embroidery on wooden chairs.
I was stuck. I was theirs to gnaw on.

In her bedroom Madeleine
force-fed me long division,
smelly yoghurt, bragging
stories, and bullied her hissing
cat into biting. Finally, she was
bored and we slept
without giggles.

Madeleine's mother woke us
with stewed prunes disgusting
and they gave me bend-the-chins-down smiles
that said I didn't know
what was good.

Just before I could leave
her mother tied a monster
scarf on my head, supposed to
cover my hair but it crumpled
round my feet, wiped my boots
when I said goodbye, fell
in the gutter by the car
and I was so ashamed I pretended
nothing happened by twirling and
slipping on the scarf once more.

With their fire-breath smiles
they asked about my ballet lessons
and begged my mother to let me spend
the night again next weekend.
I was sick in the car.

## LOVE 1 MUSE 0 *(for Jay)*

You're staring at me again.

All over your eyes smile bulbs
pop so bright that the light
flashes clear through my closed lids.

What do you see that makes
you so damn happy with me?

In the small thick hours
when my lashes are glued
together with sandy goo,
my anxious squally nightmares —
sweetmeats for my black work
with the White Goddess —
are once again lost in kisses.

## Cleaning Up

Scraping the burned rice
off the bottom of the pot
I think of you kindly.

At 6:23 p.m. — an unromantic hour
to be sure, and you
were always so romantic,
clad only in my new baby
spit up-bathrobe, post-
partum pot, milk heavy
breasts and thick ankle
socks —

I smile at sixteen
year old compliments
resurrected by your letter today
and this sudsy warm water
full of dirty dishes
and now slippery you
splashing

and me too,

in California sun

dress billowing

in the ocean spray

(now my left breast

sprays and my bottom billows)

and tan and taut and you

beaming at your exotic prize

(sweet petite Canadian

clad in European Culture)


all past nasties rinsed

clean now and put away

by my bad memory

and your good looks.

## PEONIES

Frail
white
and gift wrapped.
Mouth-watering pink.

Full blown ripe,
you refuse to flower indoors
without your dirty friends
crawling all over you.

Fancy guest soap breath.
Broad-hipped petals.
Thick country stalk
with strapping greens.

You age like Mae West —
too many layers of you sausage-stuffed
into a raunchy gown.
Rusty décolleté drooping.

Suicide,
when you decide. Quietly
you push your petals away.
Softly your face-lift falls apart.

## WINTER SEA

All the same
you paw rocks trash deadwood
all the same
once again
I believe I'm different
you great pretender
coaxing me with salty tears
mountains of you

I eat your breath
I can't go too near
I want to

you giant's mouth
I am willing
willing to believe
your frothy foam is warm

staring at you
I'm smoothing over
washing out
you slap the shore around

with endless arms
pushing sliding
guzzling me with rollovers
rollovers

where my legs meet
I sizzle too hot
you'll spit me up whole

I'm coming
each sandy step
coming to you
each sandy step
warmer softer
moister

you kiss my shoe
lick my toes
ice my throat

all the same
tomorrow
I won't remember

## B R A N D E D

Big black nurse in white too tight
rests my naked arm on the counter,
unwraps a needle from its crackly cover
and squirts translucence skyward.

Silver stirrups ice my pink underfeet.
Nurse and Doctor look down, look into me.
To get a better look, they rest
the lamp against my thigh.

Tears and slime slide
sweet and salty past my lips.
Taste last night's screw-top
wine and the football hard
mouth pressed mean
against mine. The lamp burns
my leg — a crimson half moon
brands me.

On the way a small band of Indians
on horseback on Macleod Trail
in restored native dress. One man
with a bandage over his nose,
as if he'd just had rhinoplasty,
and one moviestar chief dropped
his arm from the reins to gather me
up on his steed. When they passed
I couldn't stop crying then laughing,
said to Jay, *God I'm a downer eh?*

Zambora the gorilla girl
from "Nairobi in deepest darkest
Africa forced to undergo
horrible medical experiments"
made her look like a teenager
wearing black leotards. Later
she transformed into a gorilla
two feet taller than she was
three seconds before.

The 4H Club Princess wore
a blue satin gown, crown and running
shoes. Quickly she tried to tie
the miniature horse to its tiny coach
but it reared up twice. She slapped it
on the side of the face hard.
Both contestants were pissed off.

Two kids on the bumper cars
doing the forbidden head on collision.
The under-barker telling us he loved
his job because he could hit anybody he liked.
We promised we wouldn't give any trouble.
*Hey I know man, I didn't mean you guys.*
The underblond barker smiled then turned
away to knock down some rowdy four year old.

In the barn a woman fried up fresh pork patties
one stall over from four suckling piglets
and their momma. I will never eat meat again.
Carnival filth and ear-bleeding music
thick on our bodies. Fifteen minutes
later Jay and I split
a big beef rib dinner for ten dollars.
It was good.

## PAPER CUTS

All you virile boys
I thought had done me wrong
by planting your saplings
into other moist soil —
you did not betray me.
I know that now.

Even mixed up in sheets
we were never tree to tree,
gashing, gouging
bark, tearing branches.
We made no rings.
Left no initials.

Only stinging paper-cuts —
quickly healed —
made us believe
at least we hated
if we didn't love.

PART TWO

*I Will Burn Candles*

## I WILL BURN CANDLES

Hannelore, Hannelore.
Your name like sweet warm tea,
like sleeping breaths, like
husha, husha we all fall down.

On Christmas Day, after stuffing
ourselves with roasted meats,
strawberry pie, family jokes,
Mother mouths your name,
recites again that letter
from your Mama, bound
to my mother like a wound.

*We have nothing to eat. The potatoes are frozen in the fields
and I don't know what we will do for our dinner . . .*

No dinner, Hannelore.
No dining cars on the cattle trains
they stuffed you in. So many —
Great-grandmama, Auntie Klara, Auntie
Greta, Uncle Salli, and Manny, fourteen,
who played Cowboys and
Indians with you and my mother

when the Johannes berries
were red and ripe and ready
to be picked. They picked. They picked
all of you. Every one.
Did you have to dig your own graves?
Were you raped first? Shot together?

Not with Uncle Leo. He didn't make it.
We know that much. He jumped the train
and Grampa Fred never spoke to him again.

Now those second helpings bulge my belly.
It stinks in here. Huge and sour
is this day. I resent you, Hannelore,
Hannelore, age twelve, in love with Clark Gable
and Linzertorte. Get out of my Christmas.

I will burn candles for you every year,
repeat your name to my children's children,
but please, for Christ's sake,
take your sweetness away, turn
your murdered eyes on someone else.

## A R T I S T I C   V I S I O N S   *(For my mother)*

In a dream I saw you
as a prism fluttering.
You had pieces of glass
sticking out of your back.

Glass the size of old photos,
irregular like dropped bottles —
water-coloured with no cries of pain.

The glass travelled well —
fragile stickers plastered
you tough as shatterproof windshield
weak as fine bone china.

Pieces stuck in and out.
Displaced like you,
broken and beautiful.
From Deutschland, Poland,
Hungary — one step ahead of Hitler,
clutching Rilke, leaving diamonds.

The glass cut across borders
and veins, bleeding through your hand
to slashing brushes, painting forms
you formed.

Now you dare not sip the wine
from your dropped bottles.
You dare not wear the glasses
to see better and not quite so well.

But you see
through your back glasses
and you know
you paint for us
and sometimes we see too.

## ROSE BEATRICE

Aunt Rose's mouth was never full of raspberries
when we plucked them from her bushes, but mine was.

She cooked cabbage rolls and her teeth
clench when she thinks about Saskatoon winters
between ice blue skies and red hot ovens.

My Aunt Rose's lips kiss me full and often
and tell me only loving thoughts and sweetnesses
when she is well; when she is ill she tells them too,
but with mouth sounds that are dead.

My Aunt Rose's eyes squeeze when she thinks
about her mother, and her brother is helpless to help.

She doesn't like to be called Aunt any more,
and Rose is her mouth and her heart's jammed full.

## G R A N N Y

Soft rubber lips
brandy-scented and sweet
Prussian-throated laughter,
she didn't bake bread
and she didn't knit booties.
She did steal things sometimes.

*Terminally sixteen,*
said Doctor Binswanger from Kreutslingen
who treated Zelda Fitzgerald
so he should know.

With charm and her two daughters
she escaped Austria by train.
*Yes, we're the Nazi general's family.*
*Won't you join us*
*for tea in the dining car?*
She recited Heine to me
but I never learned German.
She never recognized my voice
but I sang Lehar arias for her.
She never forgot my birthday.

Rheumatic bones scraped
against each other every minute
of everyday pain.
Father killed.
Mother killed.
Sister killed.

Christian Brothers
Brandy owes her a debt of gratitude.
She downed a bottle of their forgiveness
every day of her life.

I wish I could —
forgiveness
is so hard to swallow.

# I Am Judas Too

I married a man whose
grandmother was a jewess
making his father pure
jew by a jew if he chooses to,
making his son non-jew by a jew
by a nazi he is jew enough to be killed.


When I was fourteen
(and a fool)
I had a fantasy I told
at boarding school:


> (Rich jew, knew it, didn't you?
> All your theories are true:
> Christ killer, baby killer,
> bank owner too.)


*I'm half white RRRussian, half good German —*
Sometimes I convinced myself it was true.

I am a jew and I don't do it right.

I have liaisons with ham.

I won't circumcise my sons.

I love cheeseburgers.

Synagogues make me nervous.

Am I paranoid too?

No, I know it's true.

It's in my past —

Two great-grandmothers gassed.

It sets me apart.

32 year old female agnostic

feels like a lie to me.

PART THREE

*Maybe Baby*

## M Y   W A Y

Rita Hayworth was my mother
Frank Sinatra my father
and the Ali Khan my stepdad.

I was a feisty princess
a prima ballerina opera diva
mathematician and beloved
by all my people.

My name was Francesca,
Rita's one concession
to Frank who (like me) didn't know
I was his until I was fifteen.

I always hated his politics
and his vulgar showbiz ways
but he begged me to stay in Hollywood.

Luckily I got to stay with his neighbor
Lucille Ball whose son Desi
was like an older brother to me.
We played a lot of tennis together.

I often appeared on the Johnny Carson show.
(Ed and I were great pals)
and I made opera a huge hit with TV audiences
singing incredibly difficult coloratura
arias while dancing magnificently on point.
I always got standing ovations.

Desi used to have daily pool-side parties.
We were just friends but he wanted more.

How difficult to choose between
ruling my country and conquering
the world of stage and screen.

I never did decide.

## THE TYRANNY OF FRESH VEGETABLES

The parsnips I bought eight days ago
are losing their erections,
I am responsible.

My tomatoes are bruised,
battered.
I am the abuser.

This spinach will never know
the sweet caress of my fragrant vinaigrette.
I am the murderer.

Oh God Oh God.
Every week it happens —
innocent cabbage sprouts,
broccoli spears, expensive asparagus,
artichokes, Japanese eggplant.

I make promises.

I try. I buy

woks, steamers, cookbooks,

more cookbooks, and still they die,

hundreds a year,

limp and impotent.

My compost heap,

neglected and scrawny.

The garbage bag, glad

and obscene.


I don't deserve to buy them.

I shouldn't be allowed to roam free

in the ripe and rampant produce section.


I must be punished.


Banished to frozen foods.

## Rehearsal

my breasts

don't feel safe here

they push

against my blouse

done up my hair down

you see an opening

one smile sweating

under pants and

strobe light wanting

to star we

fall into one

bed bad

choice

## Habit

When our love
was gone or what
we thought was love
was gone which if it
wasn't love means that
nothing was gone but we
missed it anyway,

we kept
our bodies
above frozen
our brains
below boiled
with our daily
daily little hate
which we thought was
concern for each other,

and when our bread

mouldered

we chewed more

carefully

washing it

down with

turned wine.


Finally you threw up.


Thanks.

## Reservations Guaranteed

At the Madonna Inn,
on the third day of trying,
I lost my virginity in the Sky
Room, finding it less heavenly
than I had been led to expect.

My boyfriend's breath —
clouds in my ear,
gathered like thunder,
closer and louder.

My clouds matched his
out of politeness but
there was no lightning.
Just a young spring rain —
little red drops on his legs,
in my eye,
in the Sky
Room of the Madonna
on the third day
of trying.

## My Body My Laundry Basket

Bad smells crumpled filthy-
mouthed or stretched and starched
fresh as lemons folded in tight
yoga positions and put away
when guests come

Alone together
I heave you down
full and panting with dirt
or glide you light as airy poplin
up the holy stairs

My body my laundry basket
taken for granted indispensable
you carry the alls of me.

## Maybe Baby

Maybe I won't work today. Maybe
I'll bathe in bubbles and bite a peach,
sip the juice among the tiger lilies,
sweet orange and black.

Maybe I'll analyse my feelings first;
paralyse myself with
possibilities of suicide.
Maybe I will maybe I won't.

Maybe I'll get depressed and watch TV

Maybe I can't decide what to watch,
switch the channels
till my brain becomes wet
then maybe I'll want sex.

Flash a little creamy thigh,
lick my lips but not let you, and
maybe I'll hike my skirt as you walk by
but not let you hike me,
no way baby, maybe later, we'll see.
We always do.

## On That Day of Sex

In the Descanso Gardens
white camelia blossoms
burned us more than sun
and our love
did not distract us.

Behind a blooming jade tree
I slipped off my panties
and tucked them in my purse —
my thirst for you slicked
way down my inner calf.

That cool smoggy dirty morning
we went to the rich Californian's land
and paid our five bucks to see his fertile
budding among fat Sunday families and hobbly
old couples we would never be.

Under a shaded palm
I slid my hand up your linen shorts
and soon we lay unbuttoned, open
mouthed between pink azalias and birds
of paradise poking through the tree fronds.

A straying toddler wandered too near
our tree. We quickly closed our clothes,
rushed to the car, your apartment
floor, and taking our time
we blossomed among the potted plants.

# First Time / Second Time

Was I only fourteen,
drinking vodka out of
Prell shampoo bottles
and each of us taking
turns in Pepe Prince's bathroom:
red walls, shower stall,
toilet cubicle small
and knowing when we came
out we were supposed to have
done something the gang could
brag about in the school
bathrooms on Monday?

Exam quiet
in that red lit square,
George whispering
we didn't have to
if I hadn't done it before,
if I didn't want to.
I knew
you were supposed to keep
your mouth open and bob
your head up and down

when you kissed.

So in that porcelain glow
our lips came together
open-mouthed and dry.
Neither of us knew
what to do with our tongues.
We kept them in back
along with our arms and hands.
We sat this way,
chapped circles touching
for thirty seconds.
I think we were both counting.

Ten minutes later Craig Clooey
offered me beer from his bottle.
Craig — strong dark arms, school
dope dealer, fornicator —
brushed the back
of my neck with cool lips
and my bones went soft.
He danced me off the green shag
out of the cork-panelled basement
to grass and flashing
headlights blinding us over

and over as we plunged
into red wet salty
moonblack kisses and arms
and hands over and under
backs and fronts rolling down
Pepe Prince's front yard
heading for concrete and George.

Monday morning called a slut
for kissing two guys on the same night.

## Send Chocolates

If
love
fades
like fresh
cut flowers
falling apart,
curling brown petals,
rancid grey juice, scummy black slime,

give me dry
arrangements.

# HENRY VIII  *(after cummings)*

The king's

been stopped by gout

        who used to

        poetry play and lead

               great armies

and destroy onetwothreefourfive wives just like that

             Jesus

he was a lusty murderer

          and what i want to know is

how do you like your choirboy

Mr. Pope

# FENCE SITTERS

Annabelle and Jeffrey sitting on the grass
munching breadsticks, licking fingers,
poking toes through squares of fence.

Me and nobody squatting on the other side
not licking breadsticks, not munching fingers,
not liking Annabelle's big fat face.

Breadstick waving, wet lips flapping,
yapping on and on:

*We played house together,*
*we ate strawberries,*
*we watched TV all day long.*

Jeffrey yawning, Jeffrey standing,
Jeffrey coming to climb my fence.

*Want another breadstick Jeffrey?*

Jeffrey sits, munches, licks.
Annabelle smiles, smiles, smiles.

Me chewing cheeks and tongue and teeth.
Me digging dirt and hate and stones.

She spitting mud and coughing pebbles.
Me smiling, smiling, smiling.

# HELEN'S SISTER

In the eye of Virgil's bloody storms
I am not. Like Helen I hide
in the shadows of every burning Troy,
awaiting Trojan rage and Greek revenge.
Unlike Helen I thrive on them,
thirsting for the destruction of both,
a grinning, wriggling goddess.

I muffle the crunch of sword through bone:
I am Muzak.
I freshen the stench of death.
I am spearmint.
Calm and senseless:
You are mine.

Shock me!
Come and get me!
Slumber-Party-Slasher-Films, Rock
Video-Rape-Dances — Fatten me right up!

Your slack-tongued children watch me.
They watch and watch and
I'm pleased to inform you that from now on
they are mine.

## THE SHAPE OF THE LOCK

In the beginning we were bald
and our mothers were embarrassed.

Our heads were hidden in frilly hats,
preferably pink.

As soon as there was hair
enough to clump in tiny
fists and feet,
we gathered in taut tails and whirling
twists all tied with lacy
strings and heart shaped clips and velvet
ribbons that matched our bibs and mothers
and others came and fussed.

In the middle our mothers got weird
and we were embarrassed.

As soon as their hair
was "done" and we saw and smelled it
sprayed and teased and dyed and born
again in baptismal blonde rinses
we winced and vowed never ever
would we tamper with our hair.

But in the middle there were also boys
and we were all embarrassed.

As soon as there was hair
enough to flip we flipped a lot
hoping to be breezy-busy and popular,
we fluffed occasionally to be thoughtful
and popular, and
we slowly stroked
to be sexy
and popular.

If some guy said he loved our hair
we kept it exactly as it was.
If some guy said he loved long hair
we grew it.
And for the guys who liked tumbling down
tied up hair
we put in pins with such skill
that they fell with one toss of our head
when the time to let our hair down came.

When the time to let our hair down came
we blew it dry and rolled and permed
while boning up on Feminine Mystiques

and Cinderella Complexes with squeezed
lemon juice on our heads for strength
and light and in the course
of recovery from stabilizing
protein conditioners, group
therapy and Clairol Herbal
Essence Shampoo.

We have had the long and
the short of our hair —
the layered
the laquered
the blunt cutting edge —
been banged and had wings,
gone curly spiral wavy frizzy fried,
been ironed sculpted stripped
and Sassooned.

We have been streaked and highlighted
and softened blonded blacked
and prayed we would not go blue
like our mothers sometimes do.

In the end
we split.

## PLANTING

Hungering for heat
I fall on my knees in cold autumn
and dig deep graves for tulip bulbs.

When they were brought
to her hospital bed,
Sylvia Plath thought
tulips were too red.
They upset her so much
she wrote a poem.

And to be honest,
I'm only happy
when cut tulips
begin to die
and I smell that sweet
helpless human scent.

PART FOUR

*Imprints*

## BEFORE DINNER

We cannot
blame this on the bleached
bone bits of European males.
Not this time.

East Timor shakes
us awake from yet
another hibernation,
sixteen years of silenced
blood-letting.

I'm a hooker with a Trinitron
heart and I suck the group
with the most graphic footage
until the next image kicks me
out of bed and into hotter
bloodier arms.

The Indonesians are
the bad guys now, I think.
Slitting stomachs ripe
with new life dead,

bashing human heads against
South Pacific rocks
as we choke on crushed cinnamon.

Pol Pot did it all before anyway,
may do it again they say.
Different lies, same screams.

On the playing field the Khmer Rouge
are winning and I still don't know
what team I'm rooting for
in Yugoslavia and the Kurds are holding
me hostage with their mountain
hunger and mustard gas skins.

But what about the wetlands and the oak
and the butterflied bird my cat left
on the welcome mat this morning,
the homeless smudges in my own hometown,
my grandparents' oven red remains hissing
Jew Remember Your Own,
and the broken cow's ribs roasting
on sweet red peppers
I will serve my family tonight?

## GROWTH

When we were scared
children, we were not wanted
or wanted too much.

Now we don't look people in the eye
very well. We stumble when we speak,
laughing nervous at ourselves for being
stupid, clumsy, bad with names.

Our past is like an old candy bar,
dug so deep in our pockets it gets stuck
in the lining for years.

We touch the hard lump
only through cloth-covered fingers.
We push it further, slide it closer
to probable endings, possible
openings. We don't know.

It does not come out
through slow steady digging.
It will thud to the ground,
the lining finally ripped
apart by shaking hands.

# FANNIE'S SON

One more carefully clipped article
slipped into my bag with your blessings.
An Auden biography reviewed with comments,
underlinings, and smack
in the middle is Auden's black scripted:

> *I and the public know*
> *What all school children learn,*
> *Those to whom evil is done*
> *Do evil in return.*

What to do with this, Father?
And the woman whose name I carry
like a ribald joke slapped in the middle of mine?
The Grandmother I never knew
whose hard lessons I never learned —
God how you defend her.

Eighteen, alone in white prairie heat
with a cripple, two kids, bedbugs
and a will of iron. A fist of iron —
but only twice that you remember and
you probably deserved it and you may
forgive her but I don't.

You don't know why you chose our dog
Black Sam, as sweet and young as you,

to beat and beat and I may
forgive you but he will.

I want it black and white
but like goddamn endless *New Yorker* articles
it's complicated, needs space and time
to detangle.

There she is shining
at the box social
in a sea of saved ice cream spoons
jangling like a thousand silver coins
carefully stitched on her country dress
with you so proud at three.

Here she is taking
in four more orphaned cousins.
Whole families wound up
at your home because she was kind.
Working always working.

Here both of you
laughing, laughing forever
until she died
at fifty-two.

And again Father
what am I to do?

# **I M P R I N T S**   *(for my father)*

**1.**

Year after year

poplars

berries

birds

deer

you make distinctions clear

I swim

in the cool

water of your voice

**2.**

At the top,

steep and stubbly,

I always think of Scotland;

barley-green rough tumbly hills,

strolling with my brogue and sheep.

But you wouldn't be there,

so I come back and stare at

the bigger creek below

where the great blue heron stands,

the beaver make their home,

ducks, geese and getting there
is a wet business.

One more time you swear to sit,
binoculared and capped,
a whole day by the creek to watch
the beaver and the bird.
And I'll be in Scotland afore you.

3.
Under wide
spruce needle skirts
black-green and rustling
the new sun spotlights
last night's licks and snores
little drops of droppings
hoof tracks and soft
earth indents of harboured deer

4.

There's a crush of fallen trees

in a thistle flat field

where we once found treasure


Wild raspberries

so many and so

bloody our hands and

mouths

betrayed

forever

by only spiders

and fungus there

after


5.

Year after year

I hear

I hear the farm talk

another sense to me


I blow bubbles

to make it last longer

## WAITING FOR DADDY

Waiting for Daddy
after whacking my sister in the eye
with the ping-pong racket
'cause she didn't let me win.

Daddy Daddy Daddy home!
Up in huge hugs, longside barrel
of Kentucky Fried Chicken, he calls
me his princess, his beauty,
his sweetbabyboy.

*Look what your princess did*
*to my eye, Dad.*
*Shouldn't have gotten in her way,*
*old girl!*

Waiting for Daddy
after apple juice and saltines,
Play-Doh and numbers but before
quiet time and clean-up,
hope I smell Old Spice, can reach
my coat hook and race to his face.

Waiting for Daddy
to drive me from parties to movies
to discipline me ever. Never.

Napping beforehand, shouldn't be tired,
cried all morning about my big fat body,
sung "Summertime" in the shower, wept,
waiting for Daddy to go to the Market.

Everything ready: five bags,
(they like you to bring your own)
and lots of small change. Think of stories
to make him laugh. Know he'll say
I've never looked better —
should look so good.

Think I'm too tired to drive.
Know he shouldn't. All seventy-seven
years of him, still strong and handsome,
soft light brown eyes, white wispy hair.
*Who wants fat hair?*

Waiting for Daddy's
big old man car; silver Crown Victoria,

petrified moth on the back dash,
cruise control, electric everything
square and heavy.
*I buy by the ton, much safer to drive.*
But he isn't. Slows when he needn't,
stops and goes, forgets to wink,
halts on greens. We can't
start real talk till we get there.

The Ukrainian food lady
knows us now, asks how we are.
Waiting for Daddy while he pays
I sit down so I won't try
to get in there and hear
for him when he doesn't hear right.

Waiting for Daddy
to plunk down the plates,
*What a pretty Slav face,*
as I tackle perogies dripping
buttered onions and sour cream globs.
He eats pancakes with no applesauce no
sour cream. They aren't crisp or good.
He always orders them. *It's memory not taste —*
*prairie cold, family close.*

Waiting for Daddy to choose the best corn,
we go — so sunny and we can't understand
anyone who doesn't love a market;
neither of our spouses does.
The Korean lady's Tabersweet wins.
He asks me how many ears
and I always say four and he always
gets six and a dozen for himself and Mummy,
but when I was small he would eat a dozen
on his own and Sue's brought-home boyfriends
could never compete.

Waiting for Daddy to lug all the bags
but I drive back home. There's only time
for a spit of walk and he's limping a bit.
*But the positive thing is . . .*

We separate our produce bags
and if I don't make the gesture
to kiss him goodbye I know he won't,
waits for me to. And when he leaves
for the last time I won't know.

## HOME COOKING

I loved your soup with holes:
hot fatty beef trapped
in shiny golden nets
wobbling in fragrant steam.

Deep seasoned broth
is not enough now.
I need more
time to taste your stewy
soup of wishes and choose my
own spice and tongue burning heat.

Leave your scorched dreams out,
I can't taste mine. You dilute
my flavour with your teary salt
and boiled down stock of rage.

Your recipe is not at fault,
but leave room on the page
for my secret blending of the you
in me.

## I Am Not   *(for Caroline)*

I had to be.
The signs were there:
a fat white rabbit
nesting under our steps,
toddlers stuffed with milk
shoving for thigh
room on my lap while
women carrying big and low
wandered round my neighborhood
bumping carts in check-out
lines and asking for directions.

Overdue three days.
Bloated, sweaty, ripe,
I bought another magic kit
where pee turns bright
pink when you're triumphant
but mine remained pure
white as I held out
small dreams of swollen
breasts and sucking mouths
till two more yellow stains
bleached out.

Last night
my brain became
the butchered chicken,
unaware its head is not
attached, disbelieving red,
running so fast
still believing
I am
I had to be.

## KAMAKAZI BABY

Turtle determined,
she cranes her neck
from the classic creeping
position to stalk the room
with patient eyes.

Target found,
she beams, drooling,
rowing elbows,
dragging floppy feet
with Porgie's will
to find Bess. Oh Lord,
she's on her way.

She seeks the one,
the only teeny tiny bit
of fluff on the floor,
unseeable to the adult eye,
yet capable of lodging
in that skinny windpipe
and choking the breath
right out of her.

I am now a SWAT-team
member and a thief,
specializing in last
minute swoop-downs
on battered fairy books,
tattered clowns,
and vegetable
sticks turned evil
in her sticky hands.

Daily I rip bear
stuffings and staples
from her lock-jaw grip.

What do I get?

The shocked slow motion
grimace of an assault victim.
Injustice streaming
from angry eyes.

I'm sorry I'm so sorry.

There is no ending for this.

## CRADLE SONG

Hospital dazed
by roses and chocolates,
I never noticed your lungs —
only gentle sucks and coos.
Now my civilized living room
smells like curdled milk
and each day we turn up
the volume on the stereo
and each night dolby decibels
retreat in silence
against your strength.

Slimy squirmer,
you slid out of my body
into my home and claimed it
sure as Cortez sipped
hospitable hot chocolate
with Montezuma, plotting
the end of the Aztecs,

sweetly as Juliet
danced her delicacy
into Romeo's heart and innocently
(ah innocence — deadly spear!)
caused his early exit,

small as mosquitoes on hippos,
quietly, slowly
driving those placid beasts
into crazed circles
not able to eat or sleep.

Gassy smiler,
gummy screamer —
I am vanquished
beloved.